CALLIOPE'S DREAM

CALLIOPE'S DREAM

Poetry by a Woman

AMY BATISTA

Library of Congress Control Number: 2025916629

Book Cover by Carolina Altavilla
Editing by Michael Martin

ISBN: 979-8-9996443-2-9 (hardcover)
ISBN: 979-8-9996443-0-5 (paperback)
ISBN: 979-8-9996443-1-2 (ebook)

For those who silenced their voice
until it became a whisper in the void,
may you unleash a roar
that crumbles this false world
so you can build anew

Table of Contents

Calliope's Dream

Calliope's Dream
is the sweetest of whispers.

If you try to hear it,
She eludes you.

You need to let go,
release control,
allow Her to touch you,
to touch your heart.

Allow Her to sing through you
Her sweet song,
Her sweet whispers.

We each hear Her differently,
yet to Her children
Her touch feels the same.
Her beauty connects us,
and so we dance
to the rhythm of Her sweet song.
The longing in our hearts

filled by Her words,
filled by Her light,
filled by Her love.

Calliope's Dream
She whispers.
She whispers.
She whispers.

I want to hold Her secrets.

Just mine
for a little longer.

Her whispers
Her sweet whispers
Her sweet song

Just mine
for a little longer.

A Dream Remembered

I want to kiss you.
I want to taste your lips.
I want to taste your heart.

I want to know
is it sweet?
does it sting?
will it hurt?

I need to know.

The mystery of you calls me.
It scares me
a little.
It excites me.
It terrifies me.

But I need to know.

I must uncover the mystery,
layer by layer
if you'll let me.

Will it hurt?
I hope it doesn't
for either of us.

I hope it feels like
a dream
a dream remembered
a dream forgotten
a dream found
and a dream lost again
to be found once more.

I hope my heart forgets to remember

so I can be lost once more
in the mystery of you.

Hell Hath No Fury

I gave you my heart,
and you said it was too dangerous.
I gave you my love,
and you said you were afraid.

You'd been down this road,
you'd heard this before,
you didn't have the money
I was so obviously after.

You denied every connection we had,
every smile we shared,
every breath snatched from my lungs.

You belittled me,
you bared your heart to me,
you captured me.

You make your own luck.
I wish you'd make your own courage.

Also.
I love you.

I still love you.
Perhaps
that's why I'm angry.

I'm angry
at myself
for still loving you

when you clearly did not choose me.
I thought you were choosing yourself.
But instead,
you were choosing the same old story,
its drama a warm blanket to you.

I shiver,
then pull my anger closer,
wrapping its warmth around my shoulders.

Just one more way
we're reflected in each other.

Tiptoes

I dance to your song
on the tiptoes of my heart
a lighthearted ditty
that only you know
for my ears alone
for your heart to sing
for our love to grow

on the tiptoes of my heart
where I feel the lightest
is where I want to stay

in the approaching
darkness
with just enough light
to see the way

on the tiptoes of my heart
is where I want to stay

with you

Lost, Not Found

You said
you never turned lights on
at home.

That's dark. Literally.

Yet here I sit,
in my own darkness.

Just the soft glow
of the light
within me.

The waning darkness
beckons me.

Not yet light,
yet not dark.

This is where you'll find me.

Lost, not found.
Perfectly content

to remain
forever lost
in the mystery
of this beautiful life.

As its colors change,
I wait for a brightness
that lights my path,

and I continue once again
in darkness.

Old Friends

The Darkness
beckons me

I fear it not
I have my own light

We dance together
the Darkness and I

Perfect partners
to remember dreams once forgotten

We dance together
our bodies writhing
in sweat
to forget our heartache

The Darkness and I
are old friends

We've lived lifetimes together
each life better than the last
until we came

to meet here

Friends at last
Friends forgotten
Friends remembered
through our dance
once more

Return to the Goddess

The Goddess flows through me
Her dance calls me
to strip my clothes
and return to the child She birthed

The Goddess flows through me
Her song is my dance
Her rhythm moves my arms
my body

The Goddess flows through me
She flows through you too

Feel Her song
in your body

Let Her heart
be your rhythm

Let Her scream
be your call

to Awaken

to Live
to Love
once more

The Goddess calls to you
return to Her
as Her child
once more

The eternal Mother

Always loving
Always primal
Always awake

within us all
within our hearts

HEAR HER SONG

Let Her flow through you
Let Her love guide you

once more
as She did before
as She will again

Let Her flow through you

She is calling

DANCE

Dance

I dance
to the sounds
of your spirit

ay querido
a mosquito

I'm pretty sure
that fucking mosquito
is here too

with us

in my skin
in my ear
feasting on me

as my blood brings
sweat to my skin

the price the Goddess demands

Move

Sweat

Feel

Love

Flow

She is in us

She awakens

She is life itself

Her song is brutal

Her song is sweet

and yet

She dances

She dances in us all

Dance with Her

Dance in Her beauty

Dance in your beauty

Dance in your love

Worry not

Worry not
about lighting
your candle

Worry not
about your flame
going out

If it does
there is more
there is always more

Waiting

In the endless abundance
of the Universe

She exists in you
She exists in me

Her flame is eternal

It is within Her

we light anew
and find our flame
once more

Guilt

Guilt

Why did we ever
buy into that
bullshit?

Open the snacks
that sparked such
joy in you
at the store

Let the taste
explode
in your mouth

so that you thirst
for the sweet water
that gives us all life

Also
fuck guilt

It was a ploy

invented
by the patriarchy

You don't need it
any longer

Abandon it and reclaim your
  power
  energy
  life
  light
  beauty
  love

    for yourself
    for each other
    for us all

Scraps

Thank you, kind sir,
for the crumbs that fall
carelessly from your mouth
into my outstretched heart.

Please sir,
I want some more.

Why?

Why would I want a second helping
of your discarded scraps?

You had your heart burned
and so you turned your
scorching gaze
to me.

The fire I thought was light
burned me too.

Hate and disgust
masquerading as light.

Disgust for me?
Disgust for you?

Who exactly
is it that turns your lip so?

The cheese on this pizza
the root of all evils.

I can't believe I worried about Kegels.

I fly now above it all,
my heart in the clouds.

I refuse to let you
anchor me down.

Rose Colored Glasses

I'd never let you see me cry

These potent tears
filled with the fiery emotions
of my soul

These potent drops
that heal and cure
that spill away heartache
and open my heart
for more

Do you think
because you helped them fall
that you are worthy
to witness
their slow passage
down my face?

This ache in my heart
this lump in my throat

not your dick as promised

but my dignity and courage
spilling forth now in a blur of rose
words unspoken in my mind
perhaps whispered on my face

Your dog knew
better than you

      my worth
      my heart
      my love

You'll never know

      this fire that rages
      a love without cages
      this spell of mages

and why
I let it hurt me so

What If?

What if?

What if I grounded myself
fully in who I am
and
who I know myself to be?

Would I still look to you
for my validation?

Would I still look
to your sweet blue eyes
and imagine
I see a heart
that matches them?

Maybe all I really see
is my wounded self
reflected back to me
that prickly ego
choking my soul
helping me grow.

Just as you do,

with ~~your~~ my disdainful thoughts
of my body
my judgement
of myself,
so harsh
you couldn't help
but join in,
as I did with you.

I longed
for a second chance
one to help me see

you're not the one
who got away,

you're the one
who helped me stay

    in my power
    in my love
        for myself
    in my heart
        living my life

loving my life
in love with life

without you.

Fly

You play it safe
you're afraid to fly.

The last time your feet
left the ground
you crashed
and burned.

You're battered
and bruised
too cautious
scared and abused.

But don't you know?

You have wings.
You can fly.

Your love
takes you
to new places,
new faces.

We don't always crash.

Sometimes,
we spread our wings
and fly.

Trigger Me, Deeply

I love you,
but
I also want
to control you.

That's not love.

Love is acceptance,
wholehearted and pure.

I'm sorry

for not accepting you as you are.

What a beautiful life,
in which to trigger one another.

No one triggers me
like you.

Our wounds buried deep
within our souls

pushed to the surface
in an instant

by a glance
by a comment
by rejection
by nothing

For wounds are so easily excitable.
They call to us,
they scream to us,
they bleed within us.

For us to listen,
hear,
acknowledge,
feel,
heal.

Take my hand,
love me,
trigger me,
fuck me
deeply
so we can heal together.

Kali's Dance

There is
a darkness to you
that I can no longer dance with.

Your eyes glow red
with the demon
who haunts you.

You play the perfect victim
to the sorrows you create.

I no longer see
myself reflected in you.

I no longer carry
your darkness
beside me.

In Kali's hands
the Angel's swords glow.

She churns the earth
you sit upon

and cleanses the space
free of you.

I see you shudder
shiver
under Her power.

The Goddess favors me
and lends me
Her strength.

You fall back
through time
and space,

falling through dimensions
never showing your true face.

Your web of masks and lies
hide the truth.

You are nothing,
you are no one
when you deny
your true existence
and hide in shame.

I can no longer dance
with you.

What I once found thrilling
now bores and annoys me.

I no longer find your mystery enticing.
Lies are funny like that.

These are not layers to reveal
but quicksand that pulls you in
and drowns you.

I can no longer dance
with you.

You never knew the steps anyway.

You're not much
of a dancer after all.

Menses Cleanses

Old blood,
new blood

my power released,
my body cleansed,
my soul in flow.

The stagnant energy
flowing once more,
clearing you
out of my life

and making room for
something
someone
new.

Me

Arrogant Sunbeam

Did you think
you still deserved access
to the life
I once shared with you?

Did you think
that door
would stay open
when you turned
your back on it?

Who the fuck
do you think you are?

That, my friend,
is arrogance defined.

What a privilege
to walk through life
and expect
such beautiful things
for free

to think
they are owed
to you
for nothing in exchange.

The fucking audacity
colors my cheeks.

Oh, to travel
through life
like you.

A rainbow
on a sunbeam

shimmering through
the tears you caused.

This door is closed,
and with it
the portal to my heart.

You closed it,
don't meow at my door now.

At least my cat

has the
decency
to cover its own shit.

Couldn't you do the same?

Or do you like the way it smells
and how it disrupts me so?

It doesn't matter now.

You don't matter now.
Perhaps you never did.

Endings

I cried,
tears pooling in my eyes
spilling down my cheeks

I cried
for the death I caused,
I created

I cried
for the comfort and safety
I no longer had any right to long for

I cried
for all my attachments
all my wants,
their siren's call luring me back

I cried
for the strength I no longer felt,
within myself or otherwise

I cried
for all that was lost

and all that would never be again

I cried
for the scared little girl inside of me

I cried
for the peace I had robbed myself of

Tomorrow,
I would find my
      strength,
      wisdom,
      courage,
      heart,
      light,
      path forward

But for tonight, I cried

I cried
like a woman
who had learned the value of emotions,
of healing through feeling

I let my ocean of tears fall
and cleanse me whole again

You Took My Breath Away

I once dreamed
of a love
that took my breath away.

Now I know
you feasted on that breath,
leaving me
      gasping
      choking
desperate for
      love
      affection
      emotions
that never came.

Glimpses
of promises broken,
my heart was next.

You weren't 'emotionally unavailable'
you were 'unavailable emotionally'.
Only you could tell the difference,
or pretend there was one.

So willfully ignorant
of your beautiful narcissism.

A victim
through and through
to everyone else's actions
except your own.

As you gazed upon your reflection
in that silver pool,
you drowned us both.

What a fool
I was
to wish
for a love so deep.

No recognizing
a price so steep.

She died,
that girl
so young and naive.

I live now in her place.

Her memory gives me life.
Her breath
is my breath.

I thrashed to the surface
and broke the calm waters
you drowned yourself in.

In my burning eyes,
you saw yourself reflected.
You gasped at that creature,
stripped of the beauty I gave you.
Demonic and haggard,
my energy no longer feeding your
>   pride
>   ego
>   worth.

I showed you the truth
beneath your lies.
The sad, scared man,
not a victim,
but a weak coward
masquerading as one.

I once dreamed

of a love
that took my breath away.

Dreams can be nightmares.

Contract

Our souls intertwined,
our souls connected,
for infinity,
for an hour.

The briefest of moments,
the deepest of power,
to connect to the light
within one another.

Our souls' siren call,
our souls' obligation.

To build a life of magic,
then destroy it,
the Tower.

This was our souls' contract,
to love,
to cry,
to heal,
to renew,

to rise from the ashes
like the phoenix,
to continue.

Our souls forever connected
apart.
Our light joins us
for a moment,
for infinity,
we see one another,
we embrace eternally.

Love remains
grounded in our hearts.
The light from our souls
shines bright,
our shadows
forever intertwined.

Just Another Soul

It's so warm in my light,
you felt the cold when I was gone.
Thought I'd be there waiting,
thought I'd devote to you
like I always used to do.
But you broke that,
ended it,
and I've called back my power.
I've called back my light
and with it my warmth.

Now you're just another soul
left out in the cold
wondering why I won't look at you.
My path keeps soaring:
you had a ticket on this plane
but you were too scared,
hid behind your pain.

Baby, don't you know,
we're all hurting inside?
But you gotta be brave
if you want to feel alive.

Stay in your shadows
with your stinging tail.
I'll keep flying high
without you by my side.

Rebirth

We can never go back
You told me that
once
when I was naïve
and vulnerable
putting my hopes and dreams
in your half-truths and deceptions

A pattern unrecognizable
even to myself
despite desperation's warning
siren song,
an ache in my heart
leading me to my impending

~~doom~~
Rebirth

For it is in this last descent
that I was born anew
from the flames of my
burning and smoldering
heart

Ravaged
by your distance and unavailability,
by the destructions of my own patterns

Rising,
Reborn,
Revealed

My phoenix's cry
roaring from my heart

Renewed.

Awaken

It's me.

I'm the revelation I was waiting for.

The white horse has arrived;
atop her I ride.

As Natalie croons,
a cardinal
dances at my window.

Tears roll slowly
down my face
in no hurry
with nowhere in particular to go.

It's no wonder
I return

to my youth
for answers
I never found

within
for answers
I never heard.

In a moment of stillness,
I feel the earth,
Her beauty,
as She dances
through the sky.

I felt Her sway once
like I feel my energy now
pulsing
alive.

It's me.

It's you.

We are one,
Divine Feminine.

Our hearts beat as one
to Calliope's drum.

Awaken

dear sister
Awaken

Awaken
dear brother
Awaken

Awaken
dear friend
Awaken

Awaken
dear soul
Awaken

We need you.

Unspilled

In a sea
full of fish,
I choose myself.

As should you,
as should we all.

So that when we
feel
love for another
we know
it is true and pure.

And it is.

The love I feel for you

sits
in its beauty.

I might just leave it there.

But what is love,

if not to be shared,
if not to burn a fire within?

I used to write
tales and stories

but never words
of how I felt
feelings hidden away,
felt in a singer's croon
choking in my veins
but never spilled
as ink on a page.

We

It's me.

I found myself
at the bottom
of a porcelain bowl
staring up,
grinning
like I always do.

Write stories, he said.
As if it's so easy
to put pen to paper
to make time for myself
to pause
long enough
to hear my heart beating
to feel
and then to write.

I hope you do that,
he said.

Who is he?

Could be you,
could be me.

We all think it's us.
Maybe it's we.

Beautiful Ride

What a fucking wild life
this ride is.

The twists and turns
that a coaster
has no gains on
trying to emulate
the thrill
of being alive.

But that coaster knows nothing
of the pain
I feel inside,
the sorrow I have lived,
the joy I have felt,
the mystery I have uncovered,
the beauty I have discovered.

What a wild life.
What a beautiful ride
to be alive on this earth.

Tears

My tears soak
this tissue
My tears soak
my pillow
My tears weep
for the longing in my soul

Why, oh why
did I ever silence her?
Why, oh why
did I not heed
my own siren song?

She screams in pain

We feel her
in different ways
We see her
beneath the smiles
we masquerade
for one another

We see our sadness

and we hold it
in a moment
together

And in that moment,
we are not alone
we feel comfort
we are seen

Our souls shine
if we let them
They touch
and are connected

So is the beauty of you
the beauty of me
the beauty of us

in that moment
where we can just be
before time
rips us away
back to reality

Let us stay here
in this moment

together
even if it's just me

Here I Am

I'm cold
because the air is
thin up here.

I shiver.

But maybe,
it's you.
The cold
your heart
left behind,
the arms
I reached for
that never found me,
truly.

Maybe once:
when my heart
lay open,
a crying mess
under a dark sky,
as my tears
found your shirt,

as my heart longed for yours.

You talked of that time
as if it was already a distant memory
and not just last night.
You were already leaving,
I was too lost to see it.

Lost in your eyes,
lost in your crooked smile,
left cold in the night,
your snores
the only echo I hold on to.
Your sad,
broken dick
a reflection of you.

It's okay,
I found a sweater.
He's nice to me.
He has a dog.
He comforts me,
in a way
you never would,
never could.

Still lost
in your own sadness,
walls up
while I bleed open
the beauty of Life.

She flows through me.
She sings through me.
She'll sing through you too
if you let Her,
if you let Her in.

You have to let all of Her in,
that's the catch.
Maybe you did.
Maybe that's how you got lost.
Perhaps you haven't found yourself yet.

That's okay,
keep looking.
You're in there.
If not in this life,
then the next.

As for me,
I'll be here.

This is where you leave me.
I wish you well.
You don't need me anymore,
you never did.

But I needed you,
until I didn't.
Thanks for that.
Because I found myself
in the ruins
you left behind
within my heart.

There I was
waiting for you,
waiting for me.

Here I am.

You Know

The light flickers
the branches dance
I spoke of their beauty once
and you laughed
loud and joyfully
at me
not with me

I still feel that sting
when I put myself out there
when I laid
my fucking heart to bare

and you stabbed me
       through
       and through
       and through
the first chance you had

My poor
sweet
beautiful
heart

She never stood a chance
against the likes of you

Sorry

You'll probably know
that I'm writing
about you

and your broken dick

But you never make the time
to read
so maybe not

I'll say it
a little louder
I'll say it
a little stronger

I don't really care
if you hear
how wrecked I was
when you left me

I don't really care
as I speak my truths
if they hurt
your fucking feelings

Because you know

You know

How sad you were
to leave
a love
like mine

to see
someone else
have the love
that could have been yours

Taste its bittersweet song
and find a love
that matches yours

while I find one
that matches mine

Calliope's Dream, Pt. 2

Calliope's Dream
She dreamed of us.
She dreamed of you for me.
I dreamed of you for me.

But will you stay?

Will you be mine
or will you be yours?

I hope it's the latter.

Then I can be mine
and we can be ours
in the dream she dreamed of us.

The whispers we heard
the whispers we ignored
the love we found apart
the love we found together
and never found apart

in the dream

she dreamed
of us.

Calliope's Dream

She whispers.
She whispers to our hearts
a tickle on the breeze
so gentle
yet strong enough to move
fools like us.

Calliope's Dream
of us
for us
forever.

Is it just a dream?
Will you join me?
Will you lose yourself
in this dream
so you can find yourself
once more?

The Mystery of Darkness

Show me the darkest parts
of your heart
where your shadows lie

so I can drown
in them
and taste
their sweetness

and remember
how bitter
ordinary tastes

Such a waste
we hide
these precious pieces
of ourselves

when we can
bathe
in the mystery of darkness

Miss Piggy

Keep her damn name
out of your mouth.

The lie
you tell yourself
about
      your
      my
      her
body

is the lie
told to women
by men
for centuries

about
what we should
      look
      think
      speak
      be
like

When you hate
another woman
for her

> body
> image
> beliefs

You buy into that
bullshit
using
a high interest
credit card

to set us all back
centuries
riddled with the
debt

of not being enough
Not seeing our beauty
Not speaking our truth

Well I say
Fuck that

It is time
To reclaim our
>power
>strength
>minds

To violently protest
the wars
we wage
in our minds
against ourselves

When we
lay submissive
we are meek

When we
fight their battles
for them
we are weak

Warriors
yet again
doing the work of a man
for him

Doesn't he love that?

What
good wives
we'll make

Why the *fuck*
did we ever
let ourselves think
being barefoot
was his idea?

We *connect*
to the earth
to our Mother
with our bare feet
She
      holds
      grounds
      strengthens
us

They thought
that was their
fucking idea?

Just like a man:
no original thoughts
just stolen ideas
from a mind
more

      clever

      creative

      silenced

than yours

Silenced
Submissive
Ensnared

      no more

We break
the chains
of our mind

We taste
the sweet song
of freedom
beneath our wings

      And we ride

      once more

Insert Page Break

What happens now?
While I hang here
suspended

my whole life
upended

by the belief that
there is something more?
I am someone more
I want more than before

than the tired excuses
you gave me
that I was better
so I deserved more
of the
       work
       responsibility
       stress

The Goddess screams within me
too long I kept Her silenced

I grew weary
but She never did

She gives me her strength
as I wait here
in the Page Break
of my life

my cursor blinking
waiting
...
for the
next words
to appear

I realize

I am the writer
of my own destiny

I am waiting
for myself
to rise

to be brave enough

to speak existence
into my life

The life I
       yearned
       cried
       fought
for

this Page Break
holds
...
so many
possibilities

that
       ~~overwhelm~~
       ~~scare~~
       entice
       ~~excite~~
       thrill
me

I have decided
to leave
Fear

behind
along with you

I need him
no longer

If he visits me
he's just
a sad reminder
of what I left behind
who I left behind
to become me

Was it you?
Was it me?
Maybe us...

When he visits
I remember
what I once forgot

There's always
another
Page Break
to be made

Beware

Beware:
Feminist lives here

Do not send help

She lives peacefully
with the spiders
who weave their webs
in the windows
of her home

Beware:
Feminist lives here

She is
microdosing
her
        patriarchal beliefs
away

She'll come
for you too
if you get too close

Beware:
Feminist lives here

She is
eternally undecided
on whatever
the fuck
she wants
to be

Do not
force her hand
or she will
backhand
you with it

leaving the sound
of Swan Lake
ringing
in your ears

Beware:
Feminist lives here

More importantly

she *lives*

and she is not alone

she is never alone

The Eternal

Sisterhood

has her back

Knock, Knock

Knock, knock,
she gently whispered
at the portal
to his heart.

Let me in,
sweet love,
let me taste
of the sweet part
of your lips
and the depths
of your mouth.

Let our souls dance,
as our bodies join
and our muscles shake
with pure ecstasy
our breaths synced
our energy screams
our pleasure drinks
of one another.

So warm

in your arms
so cold
in the dark
the door
never opened
together
yet apart.

So
she walked
away,
left alone
at the start.

The road
is less lonely
if you gather
your heart
and face
it bravely,
from your comfort
depart.

The Mother

Nature's beauty
is so much so
that we are
commanded
into stillness
in Her presence

    and
    She is
    so precious

that we dare not
give
one ounce
of our energy
away
from that
moment
    shared
    with Her
    in Her
    glory.

It is in this
stillness
we see
but a glimpse
of Her life.

Teeming
chirping
chittering
blossoming
life.

Buzzing
flying
glorious
life.

Seen
and unseen.

Observed,
only
in the gentlest

sway
of a branch

or ripple
of water.

When we open
our hearts,
we begin to
     listen
     hear
     see.

The quieter
and more
still
you become,
the more
She reveals
Herself
to you.

It is in that
moment,
however brief,
we find peace.

Ctrl Alt Del That Floppy Dick

Sex
with you
was about
control

One minute
hot
the next minute
cold

The only way
you could
get hard
was if you
controlled
the flow

Your dick
was floppy

      yet somehow

I was more sorry

than you

but not

as sorry

as I would

come to be

before

you were through

before you threw

me away

then tried

to pick me up

又   again

又   and again

又   and again

like a toy

like the

spoiled child

you are

indecisive

like your

dick is floppy

But you knew

all along
what you were
doing
to me

You were
the trickster
and I was
the moon

bright
and beautiful
in your
sky of darkness

caught
in an
endless cycle
of light
and dark

the ebbs
and flows
of your moods
your whims

until I
remembered
you were just
a program

      a simple
      piece of code

nothing complex
or beautiful
and I am the
task manager
of my own reality

A simple
Ctrl Alt Del
to close
did the
trick

child's play
after all

      you realized
      too late
      the work

you need
to do

lying to me
even now
boring me
even now

Reminding me
of how
outdated
you are

Otra Vez

whether or not
you get another chance
is really up to you

did you forget?

I was
        the one

who left you
who grew tired
of your
draining energy

the way you
always
complained about

        everyone and everything

I grew tired
of you

I never
        wanted
another chance

I always
        remembered
why I left

even now
you can't
        admit

what I was to you
and
what you wanted

you said
you wished you'd
married me

instead of
the perfect wife
you found

a perfect marriage

without

    passion

    love

    me

and yet...

here we are

in the same place
we were

so many years ago

it feels
the same

you
feel
the same

but me?
I'm different

I'm no longer tired

I'm no longer
contemplating
the second chance

you convinced me
we needed

second chance
to be
second place?

no thanks

now I know

this is *your*
second chance
to be
with me

was your second chance

The Spark

What is it
about the pull
some people have
on you?

Or is it
the pull
within yourself

to connect
to someone
something

greater than yourself

to want to fill
this part of ourselves
that yearns?

There's a spot
you know

in every

one of us
a spot of yearning

where we connect
where we feel
where we ache

not just our hearts
but our core
our very being

It is where
we are most
truly ourselves

It is where
the spark within
us lives

and it is the part
in me
that calls
out to you

The Only Choice

I can feel you
I can feel your pull
Through your silence
you call to me

I know it is
more than a longing
on my part
I know you are
thinking of me
It doesn't warm my heart
It annoys me

Let me fucking go
I can feel your conflict
You call out to me
through my dreams

Even there
it confuses me
Perhaps
you are also confused

as to why
you might be thinking of
someone like me
when you had someone who
looked like her

Perhaps you are still pondering out loud
Why it didn't work out for you
Why she wasn't what you wanted after all
Why it was me you longed for

Perhaps
it is my fault

I knew
and I didn't tell you

I let you sit there
in the woeful ignorance
of your own
shallow heart

You mused aloud
like you were solving
complex math equations
meant to engineer rockets

that send women to the moon
and not a simple reality

Maybe what you were trying to understand
is why I left
a mystery equal to complex physics
yet also just as simple
as the truth you refused to see

I left
because it was the only choice
I had the power of making

I left so I could choose myself

One of us had to

And you were stunned
You thought I would always be there
waiting
waiting for you
to choose me

Well fuck that
While I was waiting
I learned

I could choose myself

It was the best decision I ever made
It will always be the best decision I will ever make

I will always be the best decision I will ever make

For the Writers

A sheet of paper
is so long
and daunting

Yet a page in a book
is so sweet

It is perfect
for the whispers in your mind
that ask to be released

Its sweet scent
and soft edges
call to you

It asks you to be patient
to wait
while you write
and hope

that your words
will one day meet
a cloth edge

that holds with it

a warmth

that a naked sheet

never could

never should

For that sheet

is just like the waiting

cold and lonely

and yearning

to be something more

Wonder

I wonder
if this feeling
of traveling and experiencing
a small sliver
of the wonders of this world

is the same feeling
as someone who prefers to be at home
wrapped in the comfort of familiarity

if the explosion within my chest
that takes my breath
nay my words away
(a feat if you know me)

brings the same wholeness
to those who prefer not to leave
the home they love

does it bring the same feeling
of this is where I'm supposed to be
this is *who* I'm supposed to be?

me, an explorer
them, a builder
me searching for faraway lands
like the ones they surround themselves with

perhaps we are both seekers
but where we seek
is the difference

maybe the explorers need the builders
and the builders need the explorers
we need someone
to build something that lasts
they need someone
to look beyond their own walls to appreciate it

but what we seek is the same
whether we realize it or not

it is a connection

and while we may think
this connection is in others
it is really in ourselves
where the connection sings
our souls alive

Insecurity

I think back to those times
when I didn't know
what insecurity looked like
reflected back to me

when I still had my confidence
and didn't realize
you would flirt with other women
to prove to yourself
and maybe to me
how charming you were

In those moments
I was proud to think
a former version of myself
would have been jealous
of the energy
you poured into the exchange

Funny
how if I said
it didn't bother me
when you did those things

you feigned confusion

Convoluted meanings and actions
were always weapons of yours
a mask you wore so well
to hide the insecurity you felt

Now I'm not sure
I ever saw your true face
before I removed the mask of my own

Cheers to Never Doubting Yourself

We locked eyes
and in that moment
you knew
that I knew
who you really were
instead of who you claimed to be
who we both
wished you were

In that moment
your supposed power fell away
borrowed from the hearth
of my infatuation for you
and your deep desire
to prove to yourself
you were still that cocky young fool
who didn't have any answers
but also didn't care

Guess what?

In some ways
that young fool

was still better than you
      in bed anyway

Don't be afraid
to lose my fucking number

Don't be afraid
to forget you ever knew me

Don't be afraid
to remember how you blew it

Bender of Truths but Not My Intuition

You wielded honesty
like it was the
discovery of a new land
that already existed

inhabited by people
who knew its power
and its ability to build
connections with others

A conquistador
you proudly and loudly proclaimed
'I'll always be honest with you'

The problem was
        you didn't know
        how to be honest with yourself

a small child
playing with an adult's tools
like newfound toys

True honesty first requires

you assess the bullshit
you hold close to your heart
the untruths that
have taken residence
in the cavern
where your feelings ought to be
and you shape your worldview

How could you ever be honest with me
when you believed and perpetuated lies
created by a society
meant to exalt you
and cage the likes of she?

You bent truth to your will
at your convenience

but I knew
who you really were

Beneath the lies you
whispered to yourself
at night
and to anyone stupid enough to listen
(me)

My intuition
quieted by years
of my mothers and sisters
burned at the stake
and drowned in the
fears of weak men

she whispered to me too
at night
to a girl
wise enough to finally listen

"Bullshit"

Fuckboy Muse

You have been judged
and you have been found lacking
Be my fuckboy muse

You mistake your cool honesty
for honor and character
Well, you can be honest
and still be a douche
You were just one of those things
Be my fuckboy muse

The lies you desperately tell
trying to convince yourself
you're not that same fuckboy
from all those years ago
Be my fuckboy muse

The peace you found within
only exists under a cloud
of drugs and alcohol
Be my fuckboy muse

Your boyhood charms

turned needy and clingy
when you woke bleeding
from a bender
Be my fuckboy muse

You carried an anger
you'd pretend was absent
when what was really missing
was any true passion
Be my fuckboy muse

You helped me find
my voice
and my silence
when left behind
in your trifling wake
Be my fuckboy muse

I helped myself see
you weren't the prince who was promised
just some joke
on my path to single bliss
Freed from fuckboy muse

Coffee

The rich taste of you
lingers on my tongue
I feel you slide down my throat
My tongue touches
the memory of you on my lips

I savor you
and I yearn for more

My head tilts
and I arch my back
the Goddess awakened
Her fire alive in my spine

I want to feel this
all of you
all day
every day

I reach for you
I love how you are
smooth and hard
in all the right places

I bring you closer
My impatience for you
makes me dip my head down
to meet you

I'm almost there
meeting you
in that special place
that special way
we have with each other

I pause
frozen in disbelief
How can this be?

My love
my sweet beautiful love

is gone

and in that moment
that briefest of moments
I, too, am gone
lost in sadness
and betrayal

I stare down
into that empty void

and I think
trying to understand
what has happened
to cause this

Was it me?
Did I take
until you had nothing more to give?

Just as well
nothing lasts forever

And then
I remember
not all is lost

I will love again

I will taste
ecstasy again
and the way
it ignites

my body, mind, and soul

And so I rise
to make another cup

Visionary

I heard
you can take a test
that will tell you
if you are a

visionary

And you are

a unique
valuable creature

It's true
the test said so

I bet
when you read those results
you knew
you were special
nay *better*
than everyone else
like you had always hoped

I know because
you've said as much

over
and over
and over again
ad nauseum

telling that beautiful story
like it was the first time
every time

fingers splayed
across your chest
as though
you were Jack
singing to the moon
at the tip of a curling hill

theatrical
in your false disbelief

as though hubris
doesn't always find
a shining surface
to drown itself in

I wonder
if visionary men
are all like you

willfully egotistical showmen
who build their facades
on the backs
of those less visionary
but still more worthy
than you

It's too bad
really
that I'm not
a visionary

Maybe then
I could have seen you
and your traveling circus coming
or at least smelled you
and the aroma
of bullshit
that swarms you
like Pigpen's loser cousin

But alas
I only have hindsight
to show me
what I should have known
all along

hot air
like your breath
only bothers those
who are willing to smell it
and that is no longer me

Bargain Basement Rebound

what exactly is it
about me
that you miss so much?

is it the texts
from other women
you miss forwarding
to me?

recycled
video hand me downs
I thought showed me
a softer side of you

but like Sears
just a tired
bargain basement version
of something better

where it smells a bit musty and old
and makes you wish
you valued yourself enough
to find someone with more quality

and less convenience

was it the way I cared so much
to give you my time and energy
unaware I was merely an afterthought
a stopping point
to prove to yourself
that your dick still worked
and you could still dick around
with the gullible likes of me?

after all
you said yourself
this would likely be a rebound

yet you were the one
time and again
who couldn't let go
straight out of a fuckboy's playbook
before I knew or understood
how avoidants worked

it's funny how you can measure
the depths of someone's insecurity
by the thinly veiled desperation
in their insults to you

too bad you didn't measure that
instead of your dick
both ultimately disappointments
when all was said
and I was done

I guess I don't need to wonder
why someone like you
would miss someone like me
or rather who I used to be
so eager to please
anyone but myself

she's dead now, that girl
I killed her
to set myself free from
assholes like you
and when I gaze upon her grave
I think fondly of you
and all the other bargain basement toys
I've discarded from my life

Life's a Stage

rivers of sadness
pour out of me
stream down my face
like drops falling from the sky
sweet relief from a year filled with
numbing droughts and desolation

does everyone
hold grief in their hearts
like I do
heart aching emotions
released without a clear path
to trace their origin?

is it years of repressed emotions
words and feelings held back
ideas and thoughts
crushed by the weight of oppressive
beliefs and viewpoints force fed
to unwilling recipients
from a society
who Knows What's Best
and malevolently governs

the mind, body, and soul
without understanding the concept
except to know its power to control?

perhaps it is unfair
to lay blame for all life's traumas
on the not so benevolent false gods
who act at the direction of their heart's greed
...yet are we not all actors on this great stage?
some caught in the strings of our master's toys
behind a cardboard window
shouting, laughing, crying, dancing
for the benefit of others
without truly knowing why?

truly we are not puppets
though we play this role
until we release ourselves
from these flimsy strings of bondage
for me, one tear at a time

Disappointing Disappointment

I heard you connected
with someone
a PhD
bilingual, and pretty too

and even though
I did all that work
I still felt my heart
betray my mind
with a rupture
of energy
I didn't quite understand

disappointment and
disbelief
that I could still feel this way
after all you put me through
after climbing out
of that dark hole
to escape you

and yet
my heart whispered to me to

feel

allow

this reaction

to cleanse it out of my system

so I can finally move on

not with a fuckboy

but with someone real

someone who doesn't require me

to settle

like I did for you

In that moment

I remember

how great you are

at superficial connections

and conversations

especially when

you're being watched

you love to shine

like a penny

on the ground

desperate for attention

and connection

but never honest enough

to form any built on truth

I remembered how
you would flaunt these moments
with other women
to me
instead of connecting
with me
and how it never occurred to me
to call you out on your bullshit

I also remembered
how our connection
never manifested
into anything deeper
because that would require
work instead of theatrics

a penny only buys you so much
less in today's economy
even then
I may be overvaluing you

and so I let my tender heart
rupture
and accept
and remember

why I'll never again need to settle
for someone like you

The Thrill of Your Rejection

I wonder
if I'm more concerned
about whether or not you like me
than whether or not I like you

And if I stop too long
to think about it
I realize
my attraction lies in
the thrill of your rejection
a sweet replay of the first time we met
when I was too foolish
to realize all the ways
you rejected me then

so naively happy to have a seat
at the table of your dick
What a marvelous feast that was

I whet my tongue
and my appetite
on the sweaty nights
of my desire

for your acceptance

And I wonder
how long I need to sit
in this stalled storm
before I can heal
from the wounds
that light my body afire
when I think about you

Dating App Dropout

Dating app dropout
no graduation date for me
so many sad eyes
staring back at me
loneliness shines through
even the most narcissistic armor

And yet I wonder
if what I'm seeing
is what I'm feeling
reflected back to me

When the thought of dating
is enough to be satisfied
by just the idea of someone
even if you never intend
to put penis to pussy

I'm drawn back
again and again
by the promise
of someone
who couldn't possibly be

as right for me as me

In all those faces
I forget
I don't need to keep looking
for a dick to fill the hole inside
I just need to remember
I can choose to fill that hole
with whatever I decide

Perfection

I've created
a perfect version
of you
in my mind
without giving you
a chance
to be
an imperfect, real being

I'd love to live
in this fantasy
with you
where you're sure
to disappoint
and I'll be warm
with the knowledge
that I was right
when I knew
this would never last

creator of my reality
self-fulfilling prophecy

It's much easier
to keep myself company
than truly invite someone
into the space
where this lonely little girl resides

And so I pause
to consider asking her
to sit this one out

Instead
I invite the woman she's become
when she's not afraid

the one
who knows herself
and trusts herself
to choose a path
unlike the ones she's walked before

Perhaps
you're not so perfect
after all
and that's even better

The Little Things

It's the little things
that light my heart afire

They'd need to be
because that's all I get
from you

Careless crumbs
of energy and attention
from a life
spent in front of your TV

There's still so much life to live
I don't want to do it on your couch
or in your bed napping

In your bed not napping, maybe

But that's not happening either
with me
or her
as you kindly made me privy to

You want this with me
you wanted it with her
I don't know why
you'd think I needed to know

You can cut a rug
because you have natural rhythm
but not one desire inside you
to move to the pulse
of the beat
that lights the world ablaze

Life is too precious
to spend hours listening to
dreams you'll never follow
to spend one more minute
hoping you'll find some fire
to be the person
you whisper about
when the whiskey brings
your secrets to light

It's the little things
that helped me realize
I was caught in a dream
your dream

your lie
of who you'll never be
of who I'll never see
who you wanted me to believe
you were
the hope that kept me
coming back for more

only to find
a void
beyond the empty words
of a dream
that slipped away
in the morning light

Shadow of Spring

My darkest shadow
came out to play
her dark light shining
on the memories
I pushed down and away
when I turned my back on her
ignoring her truths
in favor of sunny lies

My body aches with her unhealed wounds
I feel their pulse lighting my shame
for who I am and who I ignored
in my attempts to
      appear normal to others
      accepted by others
Without her, my cuts never heal
filled with an emptiness that remain raw
scabs ripped off again and again
to the rhythm of Sisyphus pushing his great boulder

As Persephone wakes
so too does my shadow
Spring promises the birth of renewal

the gentle breeze of hope
whispers a lullaby
to my aching heart

Calliope's Dream Pt. 3

Calliope's Dream

She speaks to me
in whispers
that I hear
through the words
of other people

But She's always there
      Ready
      Waiting
for you to reach your hand
and hold Her loving heart

Calliope's Dream
is for Her song
to be sung

A song of
      beauty
      death
      endings
         birthed anew

new beginnings
new pages
new adventures of
  love
  sorrow
  life

Skipping Stars

Kissing you
feels like skipping stars
in a dark velvety sky

Each ripple
touching my heart
with an explosion
that lights the dark void aflame

Liberated from Darkness

The older I get
the more I realize
I know so little
of the world
and I start to understand
the only thing
you can truly know
is yourself

And so
you must make it
your life's task
to do this
little by little
in every experience
until you reach
the end of the well
that fills your heart
with meaning

And in that great sigh
of emptiness

you will find yourself

reflected

in the people and memories

you hold dear

and the feelings

that spark your heart alive

in this shining light

you find within yourself

you will see

your purest form

      Revealed

      Illuminated

      Liberated

from darkness

The Deep

Most people think you drown
but you can get lost too
in an ocean
of shrouded truths
and cloudy lies

the weight of the world

as above
so below

and so we sink
forgetting
this is not
what we came here to do

for when we carry
the weight of others
we lose the ability
to see clearly
to feel clearly
to manage
our compassion and empathy

come back
to this moment
with me

what is in front of you
that is your truth
do not trade yours
for someone else's
you are meant to live your life
not the pain of others

this is where you find yourself
only then
can you explore your depths
and rise to the surface
as you please

Sea of Emptiness

I think about all the ways
I made myself small for you
a dimmed light
still shines weakly
with the glow of confusion
over who you should be
versus who you really are

how flattering
the soft glimmer
of my sadness
must have looked
on your handsome face

my own heart ached
in the wake of the failure
of never being
who you thought you deserved
your happiness
too great a burden
for me to cultivate and carry

yet it never occurred to me

that it might not be
my responsibility
to spark the light
inside of you

perhaps
that's where my light went
harvested
from your willing donor

so eager to please
and make up
for all the ways
I failed you

believing the same lie
hoping
that one person's happiness
would be enough for two
when really
it left us both empty inside

we didn't know then
the only way to find yourself
was to drown in that sea of emptiness

a baptism of rebirth
rising alone
to begin anew

Servant

I shared my lines with you
and you snorted them
high on the judgement
of your critical nature

as if you could understand
the complex layers of my heart
yet another way
you tried to shrink me down
calling out my typos
from the screen of your phone

eager to show me
how clever you were
ignoring my voice
in favor of yours

the problem with sharing your heart
with some people
is the careless way
they caress their ego
with the folded wounds
of your desire to please them

it is here
       in this shocking light
that you see how
your need for validation
has made you
       a servant
to the opinions of others
diminishing your own voice
for the loveless words
of someone who knows better
those who reflect
the self-criticism
you forgot to
forgive yourself for

and so
as with all mortal wounds
you are given an opportunity
to bleed out
with the trauma
       of being misunderstood
or to heal your fragile ego
with the knowledge that
       you are stronger
than anyone's opinion of you

inviting resilience
to fill the cracks
of the heart
you fractured
for undeserving fools

Trippin on Roads

a dream awaits
the road is calling
  whispering to the joy
in your heart
yearning to be unleashed

the light is always soft
romantic strings in your soul
play a sweet song
  a comfort
to the frenzy
of deadlines
real or imagined

you brought too much
you only ever need yourself
and a heart for adventure

and so like a great wanderer
your rituals complete
you embark on your journey
exchanging the familiar
for the unfamiliar

yet still driving towards your home

for this road is where
    your heart sings
and you truly feel alive

You

you
you make me feel
like I did
all those years ago
like I always used to
when I was left
with the memories
of being scared and alone
       or worse
and the feelings
of how the people who love you
can hurt you the most

maybe
it was a testament
to how much I cared
that you were able
to cut me open
so deeply
and expose
all my unhealed wounds

A Woman with Confidence

I love a woman with confidence
you once told me
Nothing is less sexy
than a woman without it

said the white man
to the brown woman

society is designed
        to cater to your needs
        to coddle your ego
        to boost your fucking confidence
so high
that you have
no concept
of how it shatters
some people into oblivion

even you
as woke as you might be
or you think you are

have no idea

what it means
to live in a world
designed to
  shame
  silence
  imprison
you

with impossible ideals
meant to eradicate
that confidence
you find so sexy

a world where
skinny girls are told
  they're fat
smart girls are told
  they're stupid
kind girls are told
  they're weak
beautiful girls are told
  they're worthless

and these girls
grow into women
who are forced

to listen
to arrogant men
telling them
they're unworthy
by being the only thing
they're allowed to become

as if every woman
is not
a fucking survivor
of the
      oppressive patriarchal regime
invading her
      mind
      body
      soul
at birth

so the next time
you want to talk
to a woman
about her
      fucking confidence
think twice

better yet

think once

and shut your damn mouth

before we rise up

and shut it for you

A Moment of Peace

there is a bench in every park
where the world
slips away
and you are portaled
to a place

where the breeze
is gentle
and the birds sing
songs that echo
in the corners
of your heart

drowning out
the sighs and groans
of man's machines
grunting around you
where you forget
just for a moment
that you don't need
to struggle
and you can just
exist in peace

Frozen

I stand
at your doorstep
and I pause
frozen
by my fear
of your rejection

I raise my hand
to my heart
and call
on the strength
I know I have
to survive
any tragedy
that might befall me
for taking a chance
on your smile

I take a breath
and knock

the door opens
and your sweet smile

lifts me
out of the darkness
into your arms

Kitty Buffet

Do you like that?

he asked

as he smacked his lips

on mine

repeatedly

looking up

so eagerly

from between my legs

as a matter of fact

I did not

and yet

I did not have the heart

to tell him

and so

I lied

the same lie

so many of us

tell others

and ourselves

when really

I wanted to tell him to

      bury his face

      and eat that shit

like he was recovering

from a hunger strike

protesting

all the women

who need to lie

to men

who want to receive

praise for tricks

that do not please

instead of doing the work

of eating that fine kitty buffet

and not spilling a drop

Night-Night Gummies

I always sleep
a little deeper
when I have spilled
the blood
of my former lovers
with words
that cut deeply
to the truth
of their inadequacies

Too Soon

regardless of how
I feel
about you
it's too early to tell
if you will break my heart
or if I'll be the one
to do it again

Unleash the Storm

I'm only
a moment away
from unleashing
a storm
upon you

I want to hold it in

maybe I should
let the beast howl
into the night
     scream
her anger away

so I don't
take it out on you
and murder us
in real life
instead of
murdering you
on paper

Dark Skies

sweet croons fill my ears
as strings wail
their woes into the night

that dewy air
blows the tears
on my face dry

my hand tickles the night air
as I roll leisurely
across bumps
made by buses
filled with
tired abuelitas
working past their due
for the niños at home
who fill their hearts with joy

the dark skies
might ring
a different tune for us all
but we feel
Her sigh

as She comforts us
with soft breezes
that guide us on our way

there are those
who feel
Her gentle breath
and pause
to let Her pulse
through our hearts

we may sit in silence
or howl into the void
to ask the darkness to
catch our fears
and let them drift away
under a starless night
dimmed by
humanity's machines

living starless lives
dimmed by
humanity's vapid dreams
in that still moment
we release
and we are free

Betty Boop

the grackles mourned you
they screamed your name
trumpeting your departure
to that Better Place
as I walked out

without you

your body still warm
your fur as soft as ever
your ears somehow still holding their shape
as your head rested on
your final pillow

I stroked your nose
until the light left your eyes
and your soul departed

always my Best Girl
my Betty Boop

you gave me love
I didn't deserve

but greedily took

you learned how to disarm and enchant me
with your eyes
portals to nebulas in dark cloudy skies

I learned to gently spoil you
with just one more treat
for my Best Girl

you were a shadow of light
always by my side
even when you slept
more and more each day
no longer curled between my legs
but flat on the ground
when your bed put too much pressure
on your aging joints

you carried a quiet silence
in those last hours
a refined regal air about you
as you welcomed your final moments
of a life too short
for my greedy heart

not a whine

not a whimper

despite the pain I know you felt

I prayed for the Angels and the Goddess

to carry you peacefully to the other side

you knew

it was your time to depart

this earth

but never our hearts

for when you fill someone's heart

with a love like yours

you never truly leave

comforting me still

through these darkest days

memories bittersweet

will lose their salty taste

until only sweet remains

Nature

on days when the tug in my heart
will not be silenced
I find the road
guiding me towards You

trees with long arms
that blanket me
in the shade of Your love

where I can relax
my weary heart
and hear the soft beats
of my pulse
over the chaos
of my mind

the shouts quiet
to a whisper
as Your soul pours into me

the birds too
must feel this peace
for they waddle around me

without a care

Your gentle flow
cascades down rocks
porous with time

weathered by broken souls
who need Your healing touch

for in those moments
we share with You
our worlds fall away
and we are held
in our Mother's embrace

Cosmic Mother

Shadows lay heavy
but light bounces across
rippling water
shimmering, dancing
under the joy of a midnight sky

Long before women carved instruments from wood
the Wind created his own earthly music
through the withered branches of his Mother's trees

The stars dance and twinkle to his low cries
we are lost in their magic
spellbound skyward in the vast darkness
reflected in us
not empty but full of starbursts and treasures
unseen by our feeble eyes
yet when we close them
we see more than ever before

In this moment of stillness
we connect
to all that is
all that has been

all that will be

In this moment of stillness
our hearts open
and we see
with feelings flowing free

Unbound, released
by this connection
to our Cosmic Mother

We sway
to the rhythm of the tears
that leap from our eyes
and we are cleansed
in this sacred space
within us
together
with Her

Connected

the kindness in your heart
moves me to tears
for in it
I see the depths
of humanity's greatest asset
but more than that
I feel you in my own heart

Saturn's Dance

I beat my chest
and I roared
at Saturn
howling at the fatherless sky
that mirrored my childhood

He haunts at my gates
demanding entry
asking to take
His preferred shape
      the ghost in my relationships
that which I am always seeking

here He is
yet He requires my permission
      for the Goddess lives here
this is Her domain
He bows before Her
somewhat impatient
as most men are

and I
in my Divine Feminine

wait
I take my time
I savor this moment

for it is my hand He seeks
not the other way around
and while we may dance among the stars
it is my company and
my bed He seeks

Calliope's Dream
Saturn's Dance

      shadows of the future
      in the memories we keep
      hidden from the world
      and in our dreams they speak

He roars back
my heart remembers
she is wise now
      the hearts of fools lay at her feet

not without mirth
for the wounds they healed

I pause
I consider

this is not a dance I can decline
a King has come to my lands
etiquette demands it
and when the dance begins
we'll both learn a thing or two

for now
I slip back into this dream
Calliope's dream
and I wait in peaceful slumber
in Her dragon's keep

Author's Note

Rage. Write. Release. Repeat.

I shared one of my poems in a writing group, and a piece of feedback I received was that the person who wrote the poem (I had just read it out loud to the group, so clearly that was me) was full of hate and anger. Truthfully, I found this comment delightfully humorous; yet I thought to myself, *"Not anymore."* This is the gift of poetry, or at least one of its gifts to me: to capture the deepest of repressed emotions and act as a conduit for their release.

I found myself writing at the beginning of some of my darkest times, words bubbling up at the start of my healing journey and flooding forth during a dark night of the soul. Poetry rescued and comforted me when darkness crept in, when my thoughts spiraled, when a myriad of emotions threatened to drown me. It brought me back to life when I was devastated by the pain of living; it healed me and helped me to heal myself.

Ever the people pleaser, writing allowed me to unleash all the words that lodged stuck in my throat, for the benefit of others and their peace, at the cost of my own. With these words came a piece of my authentic self, hidden away for so long that I scarcely recognized her. This collection of poems is the closest thing to my authentic truth that I've shared with the world. It is a small reflection of some of the feelings and experiences I've lived over the last year. There is still deeper yet to go, and there are some experiences I may never be brave enough to share. For now, I've shared a piece of my heart and with it, my soul. May she storm gently into this world and return to me for more.

I often think of a moment in *The Phantom Tollbooth* when the protagonist Milo frees all the sounds trapped in a fortress in the Valley of Sounds. He speaks one small word into a cannon, and the fortress is leveled, the sounds released. Poetry is my cannon, and it has freed me.

Acknowledgements

First, thank you for reading my book. Whether you bought a copy, checked it out from the library, borrowed it from a friend, found a copy in the trash – thank you for taking your time and energy to read these words. This book contains a piece of my soul: messy, unapologetic, and as close to authentic as I've ever been.

My heart is filled with gratitude and love for the wonderful people and energy I've been blessed to have in my life.

To my family, for supporting and loving me without question, I'm grateful for every moment we've shared, and I love you always.

To my soul tribe, the souls who fill my cup, I couldn't ask for a better group of people in my life. You've always been there for me, without question and without judgement. Thank you for lifting me up in the darkest times.

To the people who helped bring Calliope's Dream to life:

To my aunties and friends, who read what I affectionately dubbed my "shitty poetry", you raged with me, cheered me on, and gave me strength when I faltered. Thank you for believing in me when I didn't believe in myself.

To Kramer Wetzel, who read my birth chart and helped me believe writing a book was written in the stars.

To Rhonda Hilburn, my manifestation coach, thank you for helping me chart an energetic path forward and teaching me to break through obstacles and celebrate my wins along the way.

To my editor Michael Martin, thank you for guiding me in a way that improved my writing and allowed me to keep my voice.

To Carolina Altavilla, thank you for your stunning cover illustration; your vision brought Calliope's Dream to life. I'm so grateful for your collaboration, kindness, and patience. I consider you a soul sister for life.

To Don Mathis, thank you for your kindness and mentorship and for reading my angry feminist poetry without judgement.

To Hannah Mosing, thank you for so willingly sharing your wisdom and experience. You showed me what a successful self-published author looks like; if you can see it, you can be it.

To Story Sirens Studio, thank you for creating a space to share words, ideas, and energy. Your writing retreat gave me a goal that pushed this book to reality.

The following fonts were used due to gracious and free commercial use policies: Aileron (CC0), Caviar Dreams created by Lauren Thompson "Nymphont", and Dancing Script created by Pablo Impallari and Igino Marini.

About the Author

Amy Batista lives in San Antonio, Texas with her cat Lilo and the spiders who live in her windows. She will stop everything she is doing to listen to you talk about the weird dream you had last night. She is adding travel destinations to her bucket list faster than she can visit them. You can find her huffing her way up a National Park trail or crop dusting her way through Ikea.

www.ingramcontent.com/pod-product-compliance
Lightning Source LLC
Chambersburg PA
CBHW031512120626
46545CB00005B/1852